WORLD BOOK

NORRIE EXPLORES...

BEIJING

Help Norrie to solve the clues on a fascinating adventure!

World Book, Inc.
180 North LaSalle Street
Suite 900
Chicago, Illinois 60601
USA

For information about other World Book publications, visit our website at www.worldbook.com or call 1-800-WORLDBK (967-5325). For information about sales to schools and libraries, call 1-800-975-3250 (United States), or 1-800-837-5365 (Canada).

Library of Congress Cataloging-in-Publication Data for this volume has been applied for.

Norrie Explores ...
ISBN: 978-0-7166-5303-5 (set, hc.)

Norrie Explores ... Beijing
ISBN: 978-0-7166-5304-2 (hc.)
ISBN: 978-0-7166-5324-0 (pf.)

Also available as:
ISBN: 978-0-7166-5314-1 (e-book)

Staff

Executive Committee
President: Geoff Broderick
Vice President, Editorial: Tom Evans
Vice President, Finance: Donald D. Keller
Vice President, International: Eddy Kisman
Vice President, Technology: Jason Dole
Director, Human Resources: Bev Ecker

Editorial
Senior Editor/Indexer: Shawn Brennan
Editor/Researcher: Lynn Durbin
Content Creator: Jenna Neely
Curriculum Designer: Caroline Davidson
Project Coordinator: Kaile Kilner
Proofreader: Nathalie Strassheim

Graphics and Design
Senior Visual Communications Designer: Melanie Bender
Senior Media Editor: Rosalia Bledsoe

Acknowledgments

Writer: Izzi Howell
Illustrator: Jon Davis

Developed with World Book by
White-Thomson Publishing LTD
www.wtpub.co.uk

Cover: Norrie artwork by Jon Davis, Advocate Art; © Blue Jean Images/Alamy Images

4-5 © ZJK/Alamy Images
6-7 © W. Buss, age fotostock/SuperStock; © Leo Daphne, Alamy Images; © V_E/Shutterstock
8-9 © Shutterstock
10-11 © Mariano Garcia, Alamy Images; © Super Joseph/Shutterstock
12-17 © Shutterstock
18 © Rolf_52/Alamy Images; © Macoollette/Shutterstock
20-21 © Mauritius images GmbH/Alamy Images; © MarkRed82/Shutterstock; © Luca Rei, Shutterstock
22-23 © Shutterstock
24-25 © Blue Jean Images/Alamy Images; © Jack Young-People/Alamy Images
26-31 © Shutterstock
32-33 © ZJK/Alamy Images; © Thewaylsee/Shutterstock; © cowardlion/Shutterstock
34-35 © Hung Chung Chih, Shutterstock; © Martin Thomas Photography/Alamy Images
36-37 © Marcello Farina, Shutterstock; © John Warburton-Lee Photography/Alamy Images
38-39 © Tim Graham, Alamy Images; © Blue Jean Images/Alamy Images; © Yang Yidong, Shutterstock; © Carlos Huang, Shutterstock
40-41 © Imaginechina Limited/Alamy Images; © Fotokon/Shutterstock
42-43 © Stephen McCorkell, Alamy Images; © Kenishirotie/Alamy Images
46-47 © Joseph GTK/Shutterstock; © vkilikov/Shutterstock; © Inspired By Maps/Shutterstock; © Kung Fu01/Shutterstock; © Haines/Shutterstock; © Li Xin, Xinhua/Alamy Images
48-51 © Shutterstock

Contents

Welcome to Beijing!

Hi, I'm Norrie! I'm a puffin. I love to travel the world and explore different cities around the globe.

Today, I'm in Beijing, the capital city of China. China is a country on the continent of Asia. Have you ever visited Beijing or China before?

Beijing is one of the world's oldest cities – it's about 3,000 years old! Many of the buildings popular with tourists are hundreds of years old. But Beijing is also a modern city. It has tall skyscrapers, bright lights, and busy industry. Over 20 million people live there today.

I actually arrived in Beijing yesterday and had a wonderful time exploring all the different sights in the city. But at the end of the day, I realized I had lost my favorite keychain somewhere along the way! The only problem is ... I went to so many places yesterday that I can't remember them all! I'm going to have to use the souvenirs and items I picked up while sightseeing to help me work out the route I took. Will you help me retrace my steps and find my keychain?

The Great Wall

My day of sightseeing in Beijing actually started to the north of the city, exploring one of the most amazing things ever built – the Great Wall.

This part of the wall is on Mount Badaling. You can get there by bus, train, or car from the city center.

For much of its history, China was ruled by emperors. They had the wall built to protect the country from invaders. It was built in parts over hundreds of years. There is a museum here where you can learn more about how the Great Wall was built.

This part was finished in 1505. It has been kept up to show us what the wall was like when it was built.

You can get to the top of the wall by climbing stairs or riding the cable car.

Other parts of the wall are also still standing, but some have crumbled. There are spots along the path of the wall where hills, rivers, or other natural barriers take the place of the wall. The wall stands around 20 to 30 feet (6 to 9 meters) tall here. Enemies from outside would have had a hard time getting over it.

Tiananmen Square

Oh yes, I stopped at Tiananmen Square next. Good thing I bought a postcard to remember it by!

This massive, wide, open square is in the center of Beijing. It's the biggest public square in the whole world. I've heard that a million people can fit here, so spotting my missing keychain is going to be difficult!

The square may seem pretty empty now. But in the city's history, crowds have gathered here for important events. Emperors and empresses once held ceremonies here. This has also been the site of huge political gatherings and other events.

This large red building is the Tiananmen Gate, also known as the Gate of Heavenly Peace. A picture of Mao Zedong hangs in front. Mao (1893-1976) was the founder of China's modern, communist government. If you come to the gate at sunrise, you can watch a ceremony to raise the country's flag.

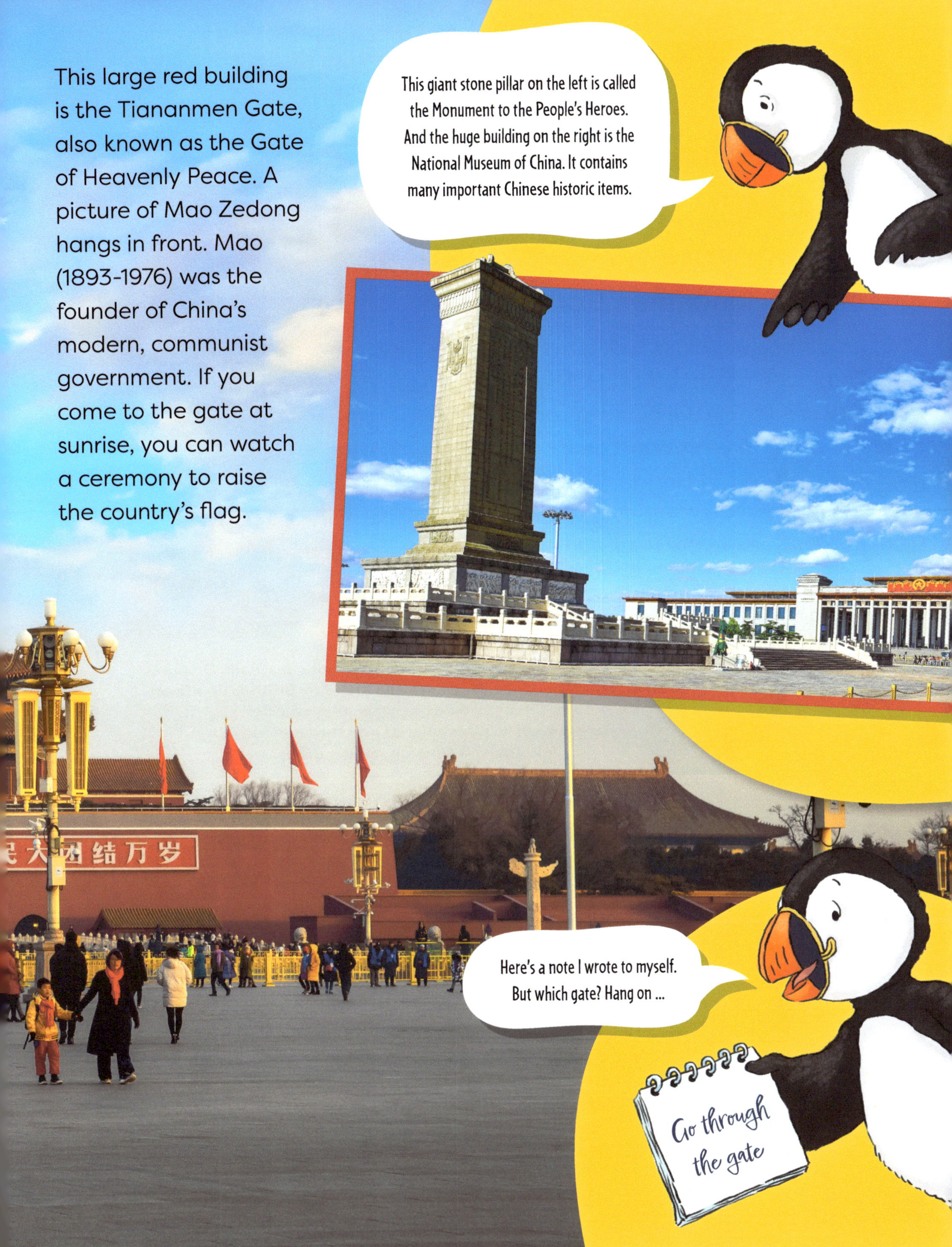

The Forbidden City

Did you know that there's a very special place on the other side of the Tiananmen Gate?

It's a massive palace called the Forbidden City. Forbidden means off limits. The Forbidden City used to be the home of the emperor. Hundreds of years ago, common people were not allowed inside. Guards would have stopped me from entering. Today, the Forbidden City is a huge museum called the Palace Museum. Now anyone can visit.

The main entrance is the gigantic Meridian Gate. It stands 12 stories over us! When emperors lived here, the Meridian Gate was for them only. Bells and gongs would ring when they came through it. Other people who were allowed into the Forbidden City had to enter through smaller gates.

Today, anyone can enter the Forbidden City through the Meridian Gate, but it's still fun to pretend you're not allowed in!

The Forbidden City is surrounded by walls and a moat – a ditch filled with water. Inside the Forbidden City, there are giant halls, special temples, pretty gardens, and animal sculptures. Maybe my keychain is somewhere in there too!

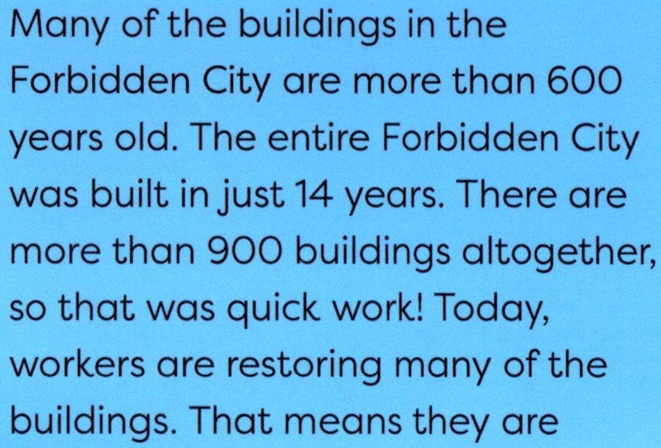

Many of the buildings in the Forbidden City are more than 600 years old. The entire Forbidden City was built in just 14 years. There are more than 900 buildings altogether, so that was quick work! Today, workers are restoring many of the buildings. That means they are making the buildings look like they did when they were first built.

After walking through the Outer Court, I remember going to three of the most important buildings in the Forbidden City. They are named the Hall of Supreme Harmony, the Hall of Middle Harmony, and the Hall of Preserving Harmony. Important ceremonies and rituals took place in these halls long ago.

There are lots of lions in the Forbidden City, like this huge statue outside the Gate of Supreme Harmony. It is supposed to guard the building.

Eeeek! It's massive!

I need to look for my keychain in the emperor's throne room. It's in the Hall of Supreme Harmony. There seem to be pictures of dragons everywhere! They are carved into wood, sculpted from stone, and painted on floors and furniture. In China, dragons are thought of as being friendly and bringing good luck.

No luck finding my keychain on the ground. Maybe I'll spot it from the air! From up here, you can see that the rooftops of buildings in the Forbidden City are golden yellow. Hundreds of years ago, Chinese law said that only the emperor could use the color yellow. Beijingers knew the tall buildings with yellow roofs belonged to the emperor.

Most of the buildings here are made of wood, and fire was a danger. Even the big halls burned several times. Big metal pots, called urns, held water to put out any fires. Some of the urns are still here.

Past the Outer Court is the Inner Court. The emperor's family lived in these buildings. Everywhere I turn there's another display of interesting

things, such as clocks or huge carvings of jade. Jade is a hard, brightly colored stone. It is prized in China and elsewhere. The displays are in buildings with cool names, like the House of Joyful Longevity (long life) or the Pavilion of Cheerful Melodies, to name just two!

Beihai Park

From the North Gate of the Forbidden City, it's just a short walk to Beihai Park (and that's where the boats are!)

Before the Forbidden City was built, emperors lived in a palace in Beihai Park. The palace is long gone, but there are other things to see.

A massive lake covers half the park. You can go boating around the lake or sail across to the island in the center. It's called Qionghua Island. That tall white tower on Qionghua Island is the White Pagoda. It contains important Buddhist objects from the past. Let's sail over and take a look.

This long wall with the blue background is a Nine Dragon Screen. In the past, people believed that nine was a very important number because it was the largest of the odd numbers. That's why there are nine dragons on the wall!
This man is practicing calligraphy by painting on the ground with a giant brush. Calligraphy is the art of fancy writing. Chinese language can be written with characters, rather than letters. Some characters look like little pictures.
See how the characters begin to fade after he draws them? His brush holds water, rather than ink. As the water evaporates, the characters fade.
This doesn't look like much, but it's my next clue!

Hutongs

Mmm! It smells amazing here in the hutongs!

A hutong is a narrow street between buildings. There are lots of little markets here where people buy vegetables and other items. There are also small stalls that sell snacks. I tried some yesterday, but I'm ready for more today!

Each hutong has its own character. Some are quiet streets filled with houses, while others have become popular with tourists. One hutong is particularly tiny. It's just 16 inches (40 cm) wide at its narrowest point!

I'm trying sugar-coated hawthorn berries. They are crunchy on the outside and sweet and sour inside!

These skewers of sugar-coated fruit are known as tanghulu. They are a popular street snack in Beijing! Traditional tanghulu contains hawthorn berries, but recently, such other fruits as grapes, kiwis and strawberries have become popular.

There once were many more hutongs in Beijing. Then the city was chosen to host the 2008 Summer Olympics. People changed the city to prepare for all the visitors from other countries. Many hutongs were rebuilt. Some of the hutongs are now protected so that people can keep enjoying these traditional parts of the city for many years to come.

Drum and Bell towers

My next stops were the Drum and Bell towers.

Hundreds of years ago, before all these skyscrapers, these two towers were some of the tallest buildings around. The sounds of bells and drums helped people to keep the time. Bells rang in the morning, and the drums were played at nighttime. You can still hear the drums at special drum shows that happen a few times a day.

There are still a few minutes before the drum show starts, so I'll check the Bell Tower for my keychain first. The bell at the top of the tower weighs more than a herd of elephants! It's 300 years old, so it isn't rung anymore.

There is a great view of the red Drum Tower from the Bell Tower.

These drums are modern copies of the old drums that used to be played in the Drum Tower.

Lama Temple

I remember these incense sticks from the Lama Temple.

This building is a place of worship and a lamasery, or monastery. A monastery is where monks live while they study and practice religion. People here practice a kind of religion called Buddhism. The monks who live here are called lamas. Buddhism is one of the five religions recognized by the Chinese government. The other religions are Taoism, Islam, Protestantism, and Catholicism. Buddhist monks, or lamas, wear bright robes and have shaved heads.

The Lama Temple has five main halls arranged from south to north. The walk through them is a symbol of the journey from Earth to heaven. All around are statues of the religion's founder, the Buddha.

The biggest statue is in the final hall. It towers over you! But there is even more of it that we can't see. Some of it sticks into the ground. The whole thing is 60 feet (18 meters) tall – so big that the hall was built around it. It is carved from a single piece of wood. Imagine how big that tree must have been!

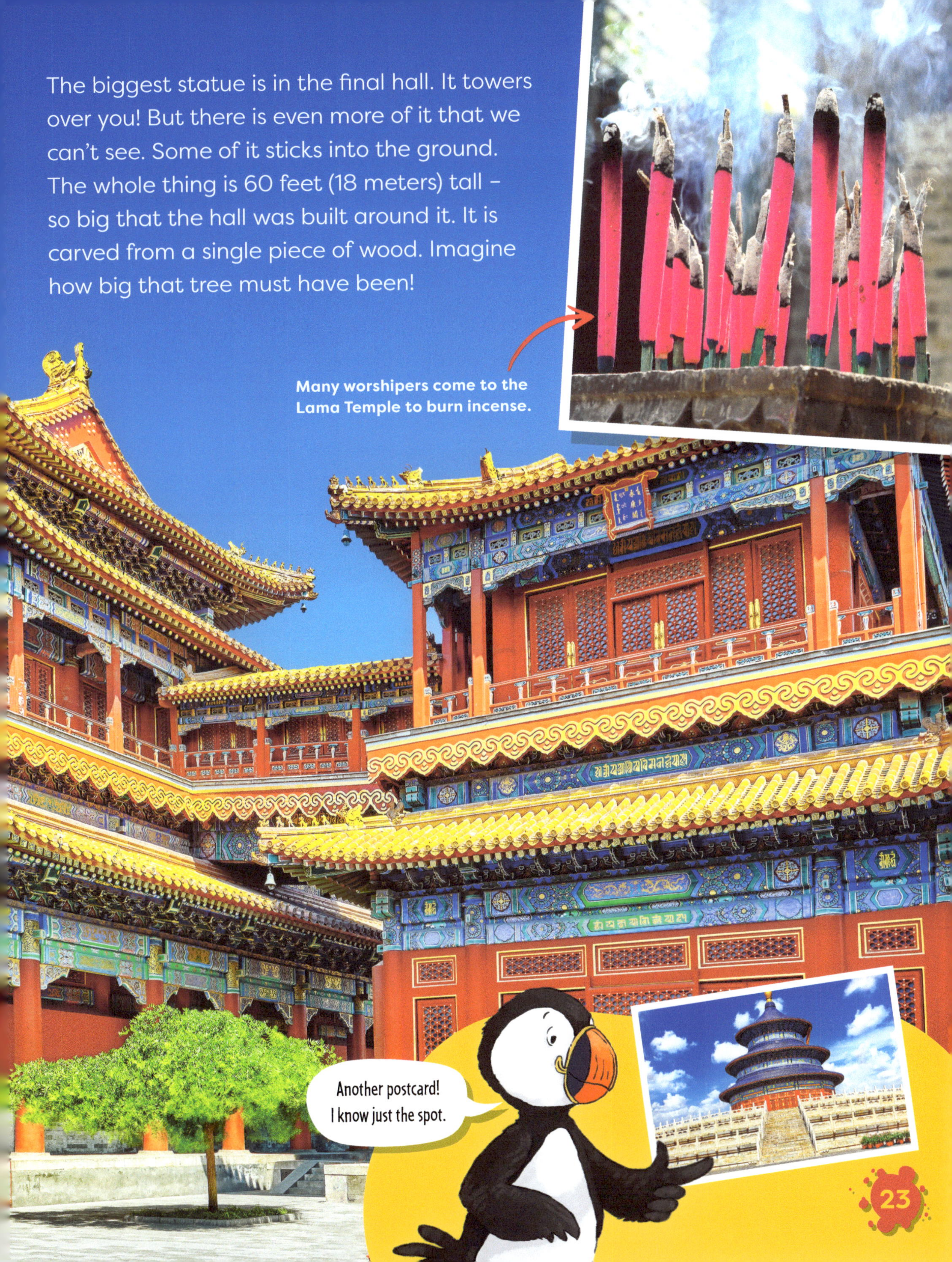

Many worshipers come to the Lama Temple to burn incense.

Temple of Heaven

This is the place – the Temple of Heaven. This isn't really a temple ... not like the Lama Temple anyway!

In the past, emperors used to hold ceremonies here to pray for a good harvest. But today, it's mostly a park with many historic buildings.

Beijingers and tourists come to the Temple of Heaven to enjoy the sunshine. There are playgrounds and areas for exercise. Lots of people come here to practice a type of ancient Chinese exercise called t'ai chi. It's a popular outdoor activity in Beijing and across China.

The temple buildings were first built in the 1400's, but they have been rebuilt several times over the years. They are a very important example of traditional Chinese architecture.

The round building with the blue roof is called the Hall of Prayer for Good Harvests. This is where Chinese emperors prayed for their crops. The emperors were called the "sons of heaven" because everyone thought they could talk to the gods.

T'ai chi isn't the only activity that people enjoy at the Temple of Heaven. These women are doing a traditional Chinese dance called Dunhuang with long silk ribbons.

The shape of the Temple of Heaven's park has a special meaning. It is square in the south and rounded in the north. People in ancient China thought of Earth as square and the Heavens as round. So the park's shape is a symbol of the connection, or link, between Earth and the Heavens.

Let's take a look inside the Hall of Prayer for Good Harvests. Everything in here, including the 28 massive pillars, is made from wood – no nails at all! This makes it vulnerable to fire. Unfortunately, the original hall burned down in 1889 after being hit by lightning, but it was rebuilt soon after.

The columns inside the hall are arranged in three circles. The four pillars in the outer circle represent the four seasons. The 12 pillars in the middle circle represent the 12 months in the year. The inner circle of 12 pillars represents the hours in the day, split up into two-hour chunks.

Look at all the colors and patterns! I could spend hours here. But the hunt for my missing keychain must go on.
A panda? Maybe it ran off with my keychain!

Beijing Zoo

Wild giant pandas only live in the mountains of central China, so if you want to see them in Beijing, head for the zoo!

There are thousands of animals at Beijing Zoo, but the giant pandas are the stars of the show. You don't need to read signs to find the panda house ... you can just follow the crowd! I'm going to look out for my keychain as I walk over to see the pandas. There aren't many giant pandas left in the wild, and there aren't many in zoos, either. I'm very lucky to have seen them here.

There's no sign of my keychain and I already saw the giant pandas yesterday, so I'm going to take a look at some of the other Asian animals here at Beijing Zoo. Should I visit the Siberian tigers or the golden snub-nosed monkeys? No wait, it's got to be the red pandas from the bamboo forests!

I'm exhausted as well. What a day!

Red pandas aren't actually closely related to giant pandas. Red pandas are more closely related to raccoons, while the giant panda is a type of bear.

Beijing National Stadium

Here I am at Beijing National Stadium!

I bought an Olympic medal as a souvenir because this stadium was built for the 2008 Summer Olympics and Paralympics, and was used again for the 2022 Winter Olympics and Paralympics. It's the only stadium in the world that has hosted the Summer and Winter Olympics! It is also used for concerts, sports events, and other shows. And of course, it's open for tourists to take a look around!

When I visited yesterday, I remember reading that the stadium is actually nicknamed the "Bird's Nest" because of its design. The thin strands of steel that form the roof of the stadium look like twigs woven together to make a bird's nest. I feel right at home here!

Beijing National Stadium was carefully designed to make sure that it would be safe in the event of an earthquake, as these can happen in this area. For example, the outer structure and the seating area aren't joined together. If an earthquake happened, these two sections could move separately and wouldn't pull each other down.

There are 80,000 seats in Beijing National Stadium. The stadium has been designed to give everyone a good view of the action.

Summer Palace

Welcome to the Summer Palace!

In the past, emperors and their families used to come here for vacation. Most of the palace grounds are taken up by Kunming Lake. Many of the palace buildings are on its northern shore. The main buildings rise up the side of Longevity Hill, looking over the lake. Both Kunming Lake and Longevity Hill are man-made. The hill was formed from soil dug out of the lake!

You could spend all day here visiting temples, exploring palace halls, and crossing bridges. The largest and most famous bridge on Kunming Lake is the Seventeen-Arch Bridge. In addition to its distinctive 17 arches, the bridge is also decorated with carved lions.

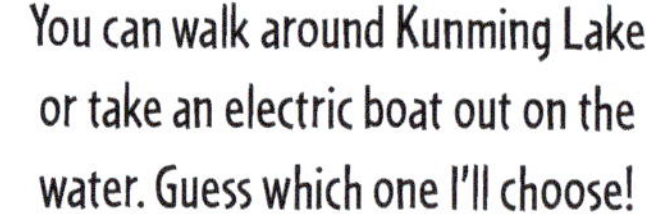

Think you see a boat made of marble? Look again more closely!

This is actually a wooden pavilion built in the shape of a boat, and painted to look like marble. It sits on the side of the lake at the Summer Palace.

The Long Corridor is like a big outdoor hallway. The sides are open so you can see the water. The ceiling is covered with beautiful paintings of scenes from Chinese history and mythology.

I couldn't see my keychain anywhere at the Summer Palace! Let's check the next place I visited. Now where was it?

Opera

Of course – the opera! It looks like the performance has just ended, so I can take a look for my keychain once the audience has left.

Opera is a kind of musical play. The performers in an opera sing most of their lines, rather than speaking them. Many cities have one opera house. In Beijing, there are hundreds. Chinese opera may sound strange to your ears. You may have a hard time telling different songs apart. But wait until you hear more of it. Your ears will get used to the new sounds.

Woo! What a show!

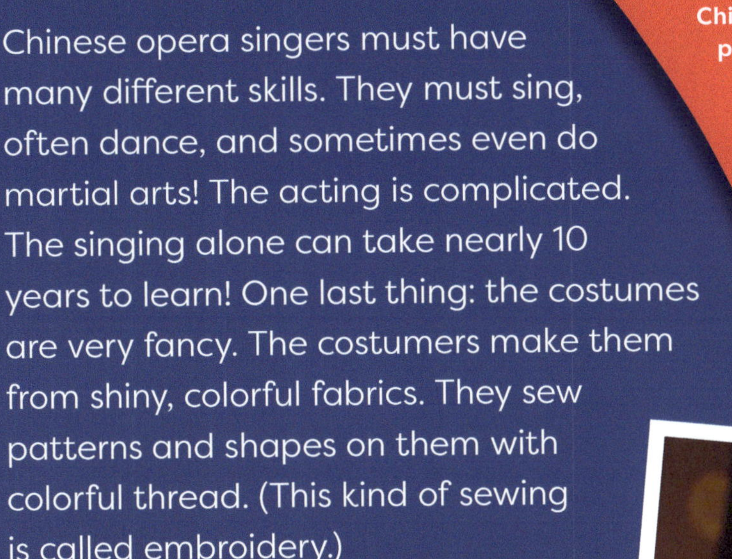

Chinese opera singers must have many different skills. They must sing, often dance, and sometimes even do martial arts! The acting is complicated. The singing alone can take nearly 10 years to learn! One last thing: the costumes are very fancy. The costumers make them from shiny, colorful fabrics. They sew patterns and shapes on them with colorful thread. (This kind of sewing is called embroidery.)

Chinese opera performers wear face paint in bright colors. The colors tell us about the character. Red is used for heroes. Bad guys wear white face paint. (White is an unlucky color in China.) Green is used for characters who fight.

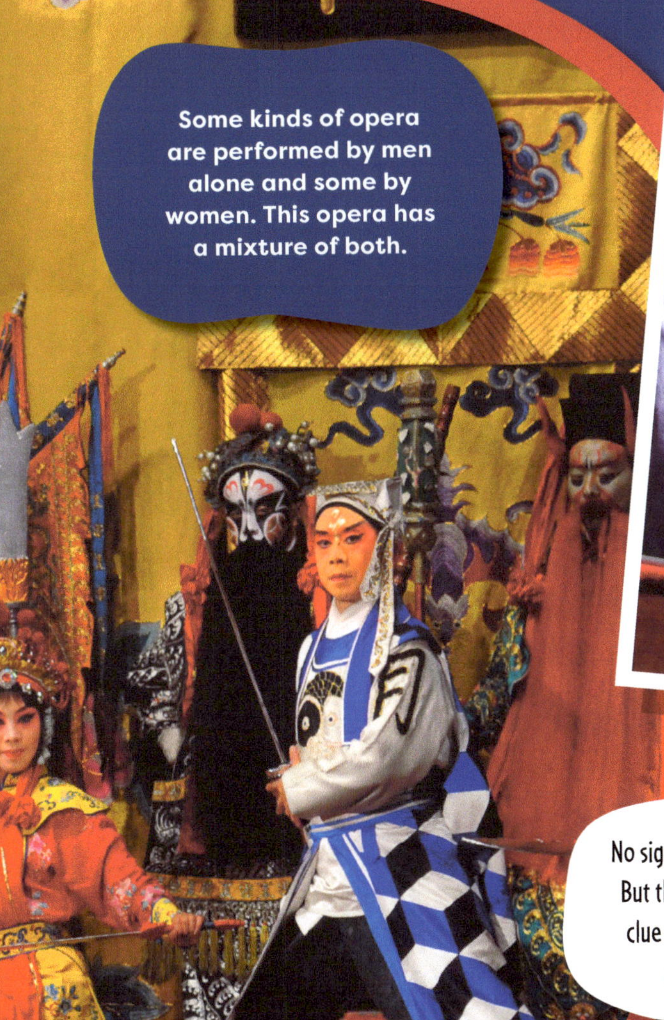

Some kinds of opera are performed by men alone and some by women. This opera has a mixture of both.

No sign of my keychain here. But this feather gives me a clue as to where I headed after the opera!!

Acrobats, puppets, and martial arts

After watching the opera, I was ready for even more entertainment so I went to the Tianquiao Acrobatics Theater to watch the acrobats.

The theater is about 100 years old. It is very close to the Temple of Heaven's west gate. The theater is small, so the audience has a good view of the show. One of my favorite acts is the plate spinning, where acrobats spin so many plates on sticks at the same time. How do they do it?!

If acrobatics isn't your thing, you could go see a puppet show. Shadow puppets were invented in China. These puppets are used to cast shadows on a screen. A master will work the puppets, while a singer sings the story. Musicians play cymbals, drum blocks, and the erhu, a stringed instrument. Chinese people have enjoyed puppet shows for more than 2,000 years.

Or how about a demonstration of martial (fighting) arts, sometimes called kung fu? In China, such arts are called wushu. Wushu is more than fighting. It's an art – like dancing, but with cooler kicks.

Sometimes wushu fighters use such weapons as wooden staffs, pointy spears, long swords, and short knives.

Acrobats have been jumping, bending, balancing, and twisting in China for thousands of years. Don't drop me please!
No luck here! But I know exactly where to look next.

Dinner

Chopsticks are long sticks used to eat and serve food. Time to visit a restaurant!

I'll have to ask the server if he has seen my keychain! Dishes are big, so everyone can share. Most of the food is served hot and fresh. The server brings each dish to the table as soon as it's ready.

China is a big country with many styles of cooking. You can try lots of these dishes here in the city, but I'm more interested in traditional dishes from Beijing.

The most famous dish in Beijing is called Peking duck. (Peking is an old name for Beijing.) The duck meat is rolled up in a thin pancake and has a sweet taste. Maybe you can try it sometime!

Mutton hot pot is a must-try in Beijing. Paper-thin slices of raw mutton (meat from a sheep) are dipped into boiling hot soup. When the meat changes color, it's time to take it out and eat!

Zha jiang mian is a tasty dish of noodles served with soybean sauce and lots of fresh vegetables. It is the perfect dish to practice chopstick skills!

CCTV Headquarters

CCTV stands for China Central Television!

This striking skyscraper is the headquarters for this TV network. It's located in Beijing's Central Business District, right next to the China Zun skyscraper. Unlike China Zun, the CCTV Headquarters isn't a traditional tall skyscraper. It has a geometric loop shape that seems to defy gravity! The center of the building is left open.

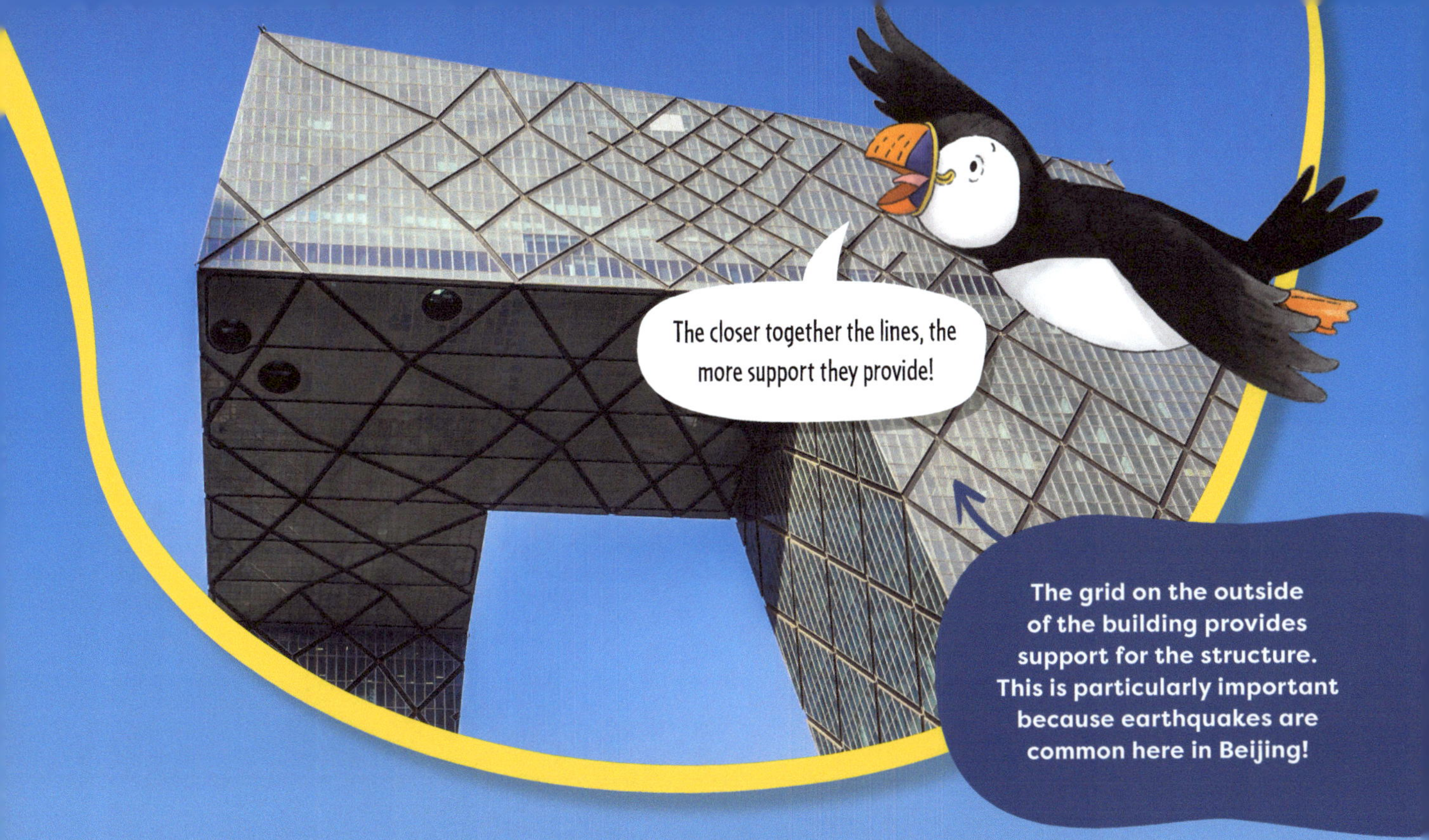
The closer together the lines, the more support they provide!
The grid on the outside of the building provides support for the structure. This is particularly important because earthquakes are common here in Beijing!

The two towers of the CCTV Headquarters were built separately and then joined together to make one building. The builders had to make the connection very early in the morning so that both towers were exactly the same temperature. Later in the day, the sunlight would have unevenly heated the towers, making the metal expand in some places, but not others. This would have made them very hard to join! The structure was completed in 2012 and quickly became a Beijing landmark.

I'm starting to think I'll never find my keychain! Wait ... I have an idea.

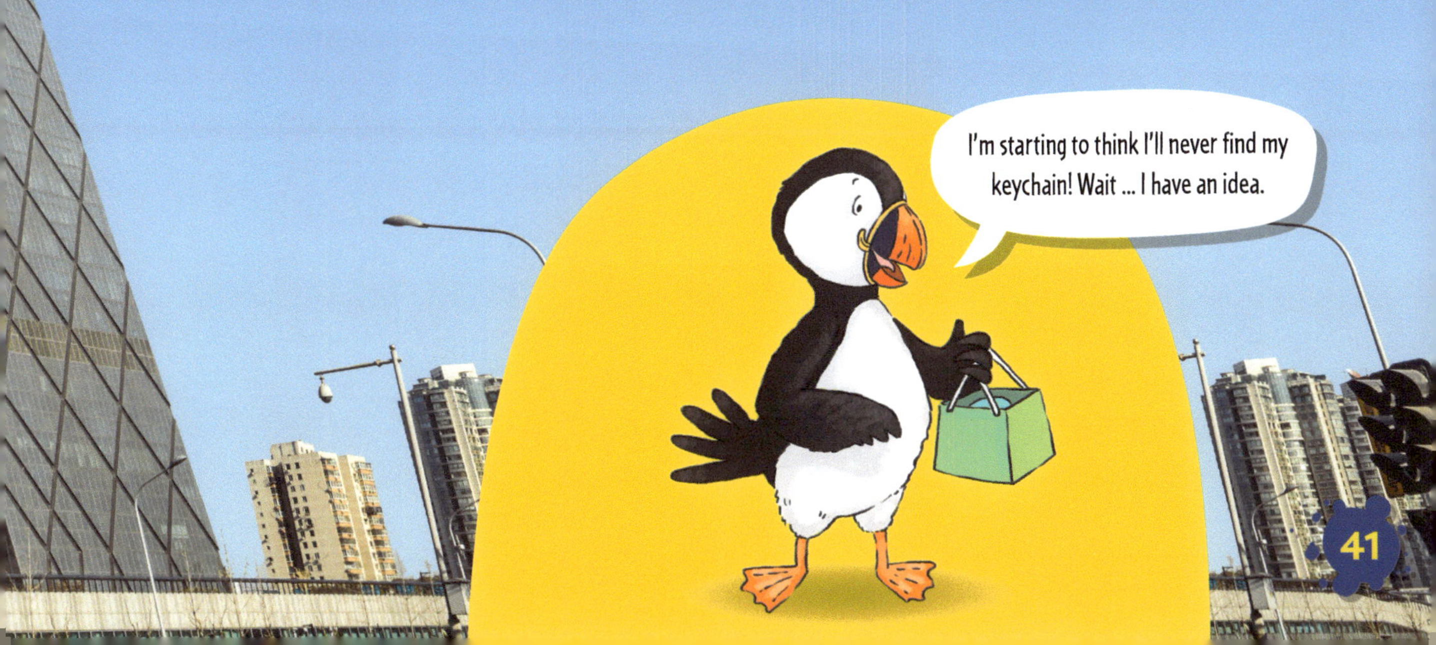

Wangfujing Street

I think my keychain is gone for good!

But luckily, I'm in just the right place to buy a new one – Wangfujing Street. There have been shops in this area for hundreds of years, and today, it's one of the most popular places to shop in Beijing. There are many different malls and shops here, so you can buy almost anything: books, clothes, electronics, toys, and so much more. Wait, I've got an idea! I wonder if they sell keychains?

Most of Wangfujing Street is pedestrianized, which means that cars and other vehicles can't use it. This makes it a safe space to explore and window shop! If you need a break from shopping, there are hutongs filled with snack vendors nearby. My stomach is rumbling! Maybe I'll go check out some other traditional Beijing snacks, such as mutton kebabs.

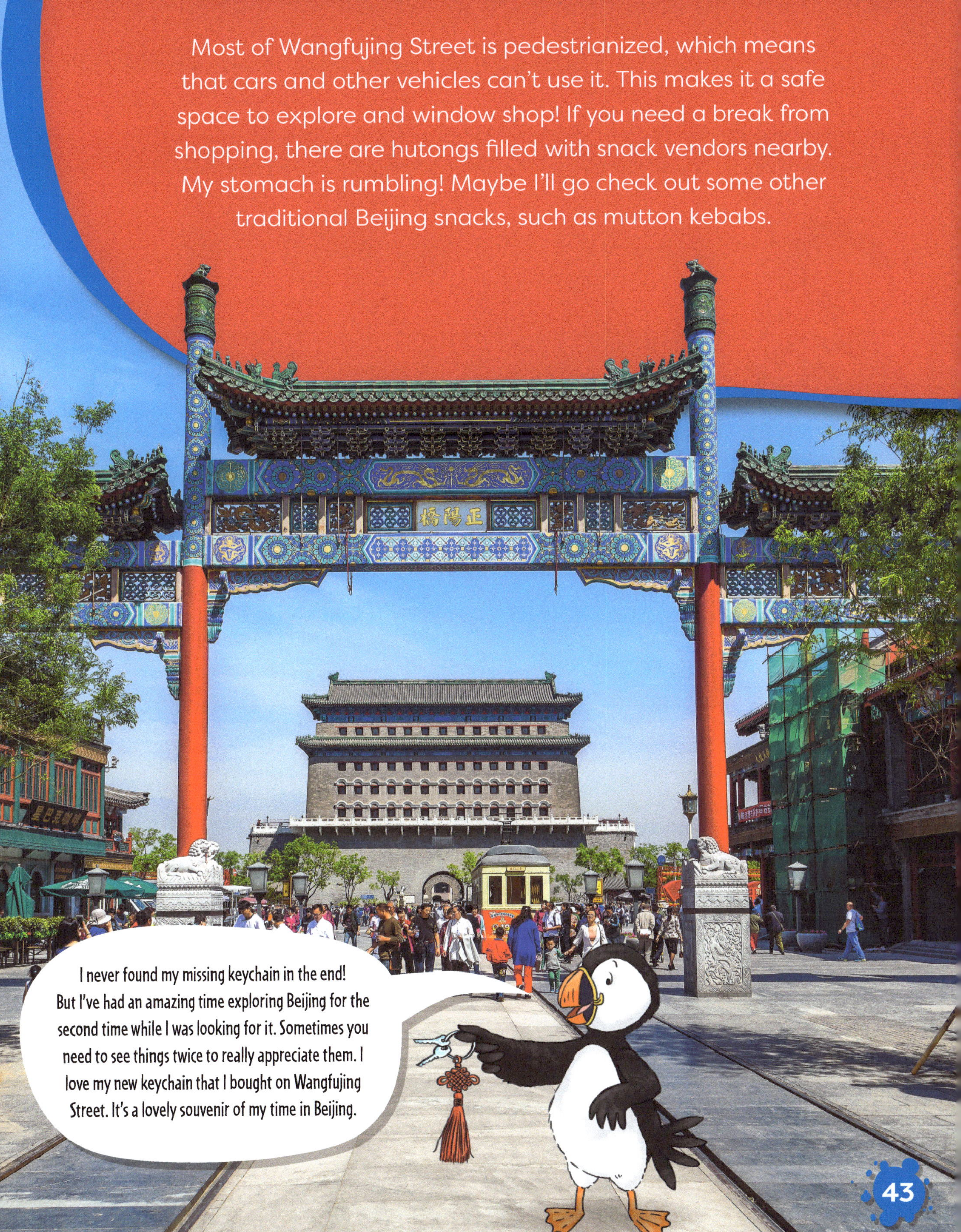

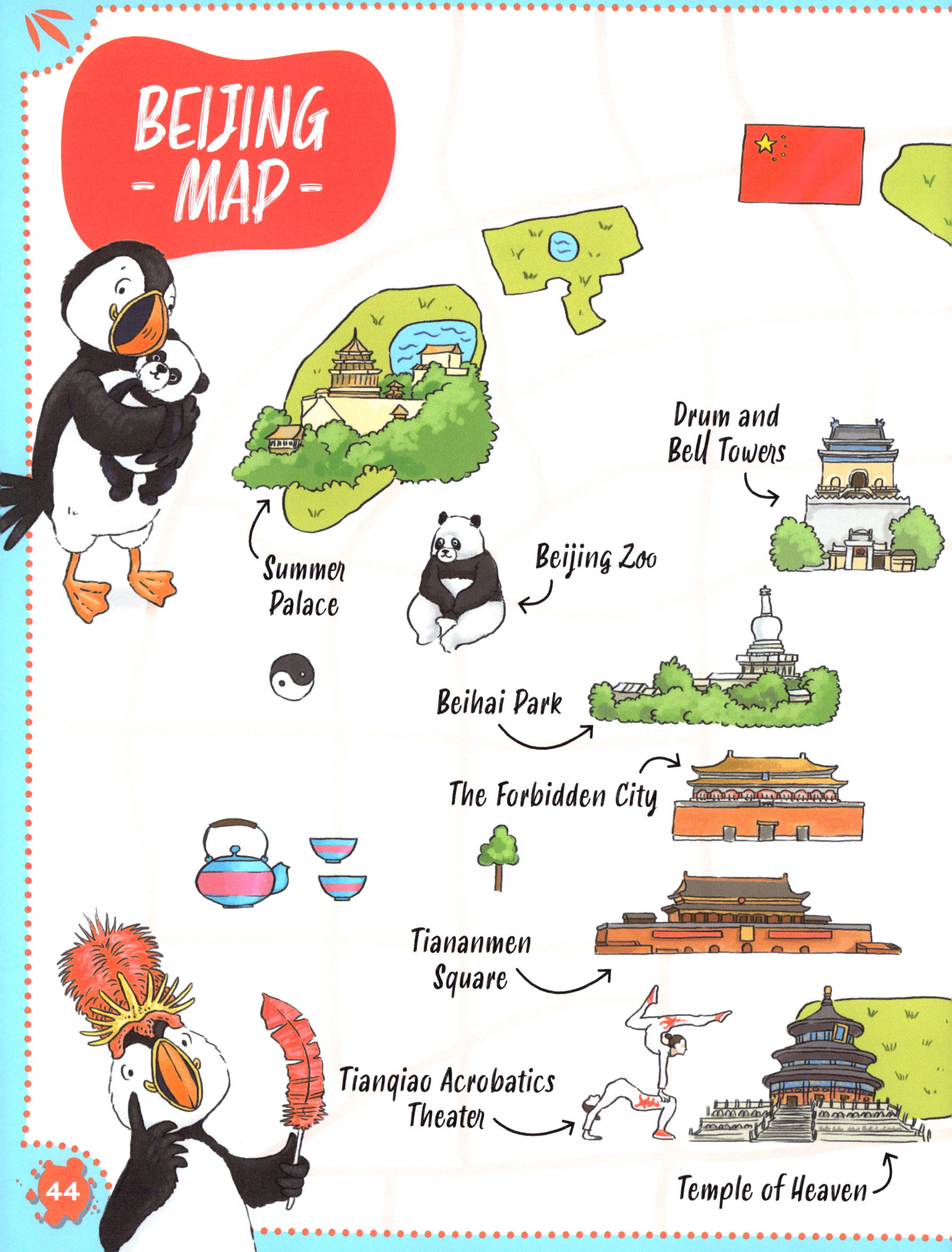
BEIJING
- MAP -
Drum and
Bell Towers
Summer
Palace
Beijing Zoo
Beihai Park
The Forbidden City
Tiananmen
Square
Tianqiao Acrobatics
Theater
Temple of Heaven

Beijing National Stadium
Lama Temple
CCTV Headquarters
Wangfujing Street
China Zun

A Day in Beijing

We have a busy day in Beijing! Fill up on a traditional breakfast – don't forget your cup of tea!

Make your way to the north of Beijing and get ready to experience history as you tour the Ming Dynasty tombs. Be on the lookout for stone thrones, sculptures, and other ancient artifacts.

This landmark is sometimes called the 13 Tombs because 13 of the original 16 Ming Dynasty emperors were all buried within it.

China Space and Technology Museum
The Center for Contemporary Art (UCCA)
Beijing Air and Space Museum
National Art Museum of China
Capital Museum
National Museum of China

You've seen some history, but it's always great to learn about and experience the culture of places as they are today. Beijing has so many museums where you can do just that! Where will you go?

Use a pair of chopsticks to eat like the locals!

Grab a snack from a nearby hutong to tide you over. Pork, chicken, or vegetable dumplings are often popular choices.

Although Beijing is known as the massive, modern capital city of China, it has plenty of natural beauty, too! Visit Beijing Botanical Garden to enjoy the plant exhibitions, scenic views, and nature reserve.

You're sure to find a relaxing spot in the Garden's 500 acres of open space!

Hustle! You don't want to be late for the show! Head over to China's National Centre for the Performing Arts to see their latest opera. What do you think you'll like most about the show – the singing, acting, dancing, or martial arts?

What a busy day! Be sure to get some rest before your next city adventure!

Where Am I?

Destination 1

Throughout history, crowds have come here for important events, ceremonies, political gatherings, and more.

This destination includes the Monument to the People's Heroes, the National Museum of China, and the Gate of Heavenly Peace.

It is said that 1 million people can gather at this massive, historic site.

Destination 2

This building is a major feature of the capital city skyline.

The China Central Television (CCTV) building neighbors this destination in Beijing's Business District.

At 1,731 feet (528 meters), this is the tallest building in all of Beijing!

Destination 3

Beautiful artwork of dragons can be found throughout these grounds.

This destination includes the Meridian Gate, the Hall of Supreme Harmony, the Outer and Inner Courts, as well as hundreds of other buildings.

A moat and walls protect this place, which originally did not allow common people inside.

Destination 4

Hundreds of these houses exist in Beijing.

Artists often study for ten years – sometimes more! – to learn and master this craft.

Brightly colored costumes, dance, martial arts, acting, and singing make for a great performance!

Destination 5

These used to be some of the tallest buildings in all of Beijing!

Hundreds of years ago, sounds from this destination rang out to help people keep time.

To honor the past, special drum shows still take place here a few times each day.

Destination 6

Emperors used to pray for a good harvest at this destination.

Today, both Beijingers and tourists gather here to enjoy the outdoor space, play, and exercise.

The shape of this park represents the connection or link between Earth and the Heavens.

Answers on page 55

Photos from Beijing

CCTV Headquarters

Beihai Park

Bell Tower

Lama Temple

Hutongs

Summer Palace

Beijing National Stadium

Engage Your Reader

Activate background knowledge, set the purpose for reading, and monitor comprehension with this tried-and-true reading strategy!

Work with your reader(s) to create a KWL chart. Take some time to discuss what students already KNOW about Beijing as well as what they WONDER about the city. You will revisit what they LEARNED after reading the book.

KNOW	WONDER	LEARNED

1. Have readers preview the structure of this text by flipping through the pages. Page 5 describes how clues are included for Norrie the puffin's next destinations.
2. Set the tone for reading: *As you read, think about all the different places in Beijing and how history, culture, and people have shaped them into what they are today.*
3. After reading each section, revisit the KWL chart. Brainstorm what readers LEARNED from this section and add it to the chart. Your reader can add other wonderings they may have had, too!

Consider these questions to guide the brainstorming process:

- Why is location important to places, history, and culture?
- What patterns do you notice in the placement of things around the city of Beijing?
- What makes Beijing unique?

Use these comprehension questions to help your reader(s) check their understanding as they navigate the text.

p. 6-7 Why was the Great Wall originally constructed?

p. 8-9 For what is Tiananmen Square known?

p. 10-11 How might the Forbidden City have gotten its name?

p. 12-13 What is unique and impressive about how the Forbidden City was built?

In China, what do images of dragons represent?

p. 14-15 Why are the rooftops in the Forbidden City yellow?

p. 16-17 What would you enjoy most about Beihai Park? Why?

p. 18-19 Why do cars or buses rarely drive through hutongs in Beijing?

What did Beijing do to prepare for hosting the 2008 Summer Olympics?

p. 20-21 Why were the Drum and Bell towers originally built?

p. 22-23 What is a monastery?

What five religions are recognized by the Chinese government?

p. 24-25 If the Temple of Heaven is not a religious building, then how is it used in Beijing?

p. 26-27 The Temple of Heaven was designed and constructed to symbolize many things. Which representation most interests you and why?

p. 28-29 How do giant pandas and red pandas compare?

p. 30-31 What did the architects need to consider when designing Beijing National Stadium?

How has the stadium been used?

p. 32-33 What part(s) of the Summer Palace stand out to you the most? Why?

p. 34-35 What skills must Chinese opera singers possess?

What do the colors white, green, and red represent in traditional Chinese opera?

p. 36-37 Would you rather see acrobats, a puppet show, or a martial arts performance in Beijing? Why?

p. 38-39 What is mutton hot pot?

How does dinner in a Beijing restaurant compare to eating at a restaurant where you live?

p. 40-41 What did the CCTV builders need to consider when connecting the headquarters' original two towers?

p. 42-43 Wangfujing Street is considered to be *pedestrianized.* What does this mean?

Extend Through Writing

Norrie the puffin just took you on a tour of Beijing, China! Based on the places highlighted in this book, where would you like to visit in Beijing?

Your written response should include:

- An introduction, including a general statement about Beijing
- At least three places you would like to visit and at least three reasons why these places interest you
- A conclusion in which you briefly restate your interest in these three famous Beijing destinations

Copy this graphic organizer onto another sheet of paper or visit **www.worldbook.com/resources** to download and print a copy. Use it to help you plan your writing.

Introduction:		
Destination 1	Destination 2	Destination 3
Reason 1	Reason 1	Reason 1
Reason 2	Reason 2	Reason 2
Reason 3	Reason 3	Reason 3
Conclusion:		

Answers

Where Am I? answers, p. 48-49:

1. Tiananmen Square, 2. China Zun skyscraper, 3. The Forbidden City, 4. Chinese opera, 5. Drum and Bell towers, 6. Temple of Heaven

Comprehension question answers, p. 53:

p. 6-7

The Great Wall was originally constructed hundreds of years ago. Emperors built it because they wanted to protect the country from invaders.

p. 8-9

Tiananmen Square is the largest public square in the world. Throughout history, it has been known for holding ceremonies, hosting events, and as the site of major political gatherings.

p. 10-11

Answers may vary but readers will likely suggest the city was named because common people were forbidden from entering, as the city was only for the emperor.

p. 12-13

The Forbidden City's 900+ buildings were built in just 14 years! That's quite fast, especially considering they were built over 600 years ago.

In China, dragons are considered friendly and to bring people good luck.

p. 14-15

The rooftops in the Forbidden City are yellow because this area used to house the emperors and, hundreds of years ago, there was a law that reserved the color yellow only for them.

p. 16-17

Answers may vary.

p. 18-19

Cars and buses rarely drive through hutongs because most are too narrow.

In 2008, Beijing rebuilt many hutongs to prepare for hosting the Summer Olympics.

p. 20-21

The Drum and Bell towers were originally constructed hundreds of years ago in order to help people keep track of time.

p. 22-23

A monastery is a place where monks live, study, and practice religion.

The Chinese government officially recognizes five religions: Buddhism, Taoism, Islam, Protestantism, and Catholicism.

p. 24-25

The Temple of Heaven is not a religious temple. Rather, it is more of a park! People enjoy the outdoors, play, and exercise here. They also visit the temple buildings and enjoy the beautiful artwork and architecture.

p. 26-27

Answers may vary, but readers should reference the text.

p. 28-29

Both giant pandas and red pandas are native to Asia. Although they have similar names, they are not closely related. Red pandas are more closely related to raccoons whereas giant pandas are bears.

p. 30-31

The architects had to carefully consider how they could design Beijing National Stadium so that it stays safe in the event of an earthquake.

In the past, the stadium has hosted both the Summer and Winter Olympics, concerts, sporting events, and other shows.

p. 32-33

Answers may vary.

p. 34-35

Chinese opera singers are quite talented! Not only can they sing, but they must also be able to act, dance, and even do martial arts!

p. 36-37

Answers may vary.

p. 38-39

Hot pot is a style of cooking and eating where one dips such meat as mutton (sheep) into boiling hot soup so it cooks.

Answers may vary.

p. 40-41

When connecting the original CCTV towers, builders had to consider how the angle of the sun throughout the day would affect their construction. They chose to build in the morning to avoid any issues caused by excess heat.

p. 42-43

The word pedestrianized means that it is easy, safe, and accessible for people (pedestrians) to enjoy the area without a vehicle. Wangujing Street is a great example of this because people can walk around and shop, without worrying about cars.

Glossary

Beijinger *(bay ZHING er)* A person who lives in the city of Beijing

Buddhism *(BOO dihz uhm)* A religion started in India by a man named Siddhartha Gautama. His followers called him the Buddha, which means Enlightened One. An enlightened person is someone who is wise, fair, and thoughtful.

emperor *(EHM per ohr)* The ruler of a large area, sometimes a group of nations or states

empress *(EHM prihs)* The wife of an emperor or a female emperor

incense *(IHN sehns)* A mixture of spices and other substances that smells sweet and gives off smoke when burned

Index

www.ingramcontent.com/pod-product-compliance
Ingram Content Group UK Ltd.
Pitfield, Milton Keynes, MK11 3LW, UK
UKHW060104300726
14090UKWH00003B/373
9780716653240